Star Glyphs and Sacred Symbols

✦ ✦ ◆ ✦ ✦

A Coloring Book for Contemplation & Awakening

33 Pictograms with Meditations and Affirmations

✦ ✦ ◆ ✦ ✦

by Michele Pasciullo

This book is dedicated to my magical children, Benjamin and Rebecca - and their children, and their children's children, and all the generations to come. May they know a world of peace, love, and harmony.

About Star Glyphs and Sacred Symbols

✦ ◆ ✦

Sacred symbols have been used in temples, pyramids, stone circles, and power places on earth for thousands of years. The origins of most of these are mysterious. While many of the images in this book come from these traditions, the majority of them are GEOGLYPHS (commonly referred to as "crop circles"). Geoglyphs are geometric designs that have been appearing in fields of living grain for 40++ years in increasing complexity. Most of them appear in the south of England around the area of Stonehenge and Avebury, but they have been reported all over the globe. Their appearance seems to coincide with the mass awakening on the planet and may serve as a type of universal language or system of information. The ones I chose to recreate are based on Sacred Geometry.

While the images in this book are flat or 2D, they can also be viewed as 3-dimensional or coming alive in space. The circle becomes a sphere, the square becomes a cube, and so on. When viewed in this way, the symbols start to pop off of the page or come to life. Especially when colored or shaded, the different dimensions become more apparent, extending past 3D to 4D and beyond.

The study of CYMATICS shows that frequencies of sound waves when applied to matter create geometric patterns that are visible to our eyes. The higher frequencies of "sound" (for example a dog whistle) that we can't pick up with our ears are still surrounding us although we can't hear them. These unseen waves are still affecting us.

Sacred Geometry is a field of knowledge that has been passed from awakened master to initiate across time. This geometry is encoded in our physical bodies including our DNA, making us living temples. With the current awakening occurring, we are invited to become our own master by exploring the wealth of knowledge being remembered and shared.

Every symbol in this book is drawn by hand with LOVE and INTENTION. They were then scanned to keep their character. No computer enhancements were used so as to preserve the original energy as much as possible. Small "imperfections" may appear as alignment marks that were used in their creation. I hope you feel their power as much as I did when drawing them, from my heart to yours.

An Introduction to Sacred Geometry

Volumes have been written about Sacred Geometry, its meaning and applications. This introduction is an attempt to present you with some basic concepts as a starting point for further exploration and as a basis for some of the ideas brought forth in this book.

Geometry and math can be intimidating for some but this is a chance to change that and see the beauty inherent in it. The word GEOMETRY simply means "the measure of the earth" (geo = earth, metry = measure). When paired with the word SACRED we are adding an aura of mystery, awe, and wonder to it. This is not to be confused with puzzlement but rather a sense of something waiting to be discovered or unraveled. When we start to remember this connection to the earth, something truly magical starts to happen.

All of the images in this book are FLAT, or 2-dimensional (2D) which is a limitation of paper and pencil. However I invite you to view them as merely representations or SYMBOLS of larger concepts.

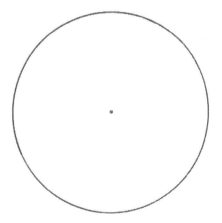

One of the first principles of Sacred Geometry is the CIRCLE. Actually the beginning of every living being is the circle, representing the single cell awaiting division or the egg anticipating fertilization. It is the EYE. The circle or sphere is a representation of the Earth, a planet, the Sun.

The circle is also the basis of a MANDALA – a spiritual drawing meant to convey universal concepts, focus attention and help the observer/creator go inward.

In the center of the circle is the POINT from which the circle emanates. It is the core of its being, the nucleus. It's also where the artist places the compass to draw an equal perimeter around which to explore. This point can still be seen in many of the drawings in this book.

An Introduction to Sacred Geometry

When the circle is ready to divide, it goes to the edge of what is known (its perimeter) and duplicates itself. This forms the next concept of Sacred Geometry, the VESICA PISCIS. The Vesica represents an opening or doorway for spirit to come through. This familiar shape can be seen in nature as a seed, a leaf, a mouth, the slit of an eye, a vagina, a portal. It also contains many mathematical constants that start to build the material world.

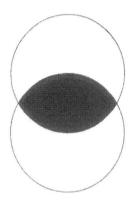

Next consider the SEED OF LIFE, an image created by drawing equal circles at each intersecting point of the original circle. Six circles fit perfectly around the original one. When viewed as a 3-dimensional drawing or a collection of spheres, it becomes the first eight cells of an embryo that has doubled from 1 to 2, from 2 to 4, then from 4 to 8.

When we continue to draw circles at the intersections of the existing circles, we create the Flower of Life, the Fruit of Life, the Tree of Life and all other Sacred Geometry patterns. The SEED OF LIFE and its proportions are the basis for every drawing in this book.

In Sacred Geometry, the circle represents the FEMININE aspect of creation while the LINE represents the MALE. The combination of circles and lines create our reality in infinite variety. By drawing lines from various intersecting points and center points of the original circles, we see the beautiful patterns of creation emerge. This book explores a few of these patterns and invites you to explore them as well.

Don't worry that this information seems hard to grasp with the rational mind. It's part of our DNA and who we are as humans. By being exposed to these images and concepts, we are triggering a remembering within ourselves that can help us expand to the next level of our evolution. Let them sit and simmer. Color and be joyful. Let go of the rational mind for a bit and just be in the flow of creation!

Suggestions for How to Use this Book

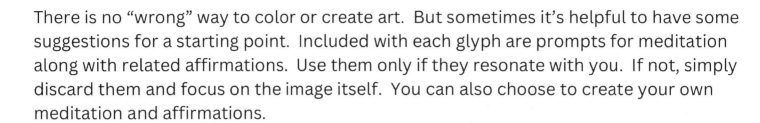

There is no "wrong" way to color or create art. But sometimes it's helpful to have some suggestions for a starting point. Included with each glyph are prompts for meditation along with related affirmations. Use them only if they resonate with you. If not, simply discard them and focus on the image itself. You can also choose to create your own meditation and affirmations.

Space is intentionally left around the page so you can add words, thoughts, extra doodles, or whatever comes through. The glyphs are made on a square so the text can be cut off the bottom if you choose to keep or frame your completed art.

- Make time for yourself – set aside 30-60 minutes (or more) to sit quietly and create without being disturbed.
- Take care of personal comforts before beginning – grab some water or snacks, use the toilet, etc.
- Grab your favorite medium to color – crayons, colored pencils, markers, or a combination (*tip – when using markers, place a sheet of paper in between your drawing and the next page to prevent bleeding into the next symbol)
- Set up a comfortable place to sit at a table or use a sofa with lap desk or clipboard
- Set your space with some calming music (I love 432hz frequency music or other soothing vibes)
- Take a moment to breathe deeply and let go of the outside world. Center in your heart. Be present with yourself.
- Set an intention – if this resonates. Use the included text or modify it and create your own. Coloring a mandala is a great way to work through questions or issues. Give your problem to the circle and then release it.
- Trust yourself. Grab the first color that calls to you or close your eyes and pick. Start at the center or the outside, there's no wrong way.
- Let it go. When you feel complete with your art, let it go. You can display it (for a long time or short time), you can gift it (release it to the world), you can destroy it (trash, shred or burn it – trust me it feels good!), or you may want to keep it for a while. The process is more important than the result. Relieve yourself of the burden of making a masterpiece.
- LOVE & HONOR YOURSELF!

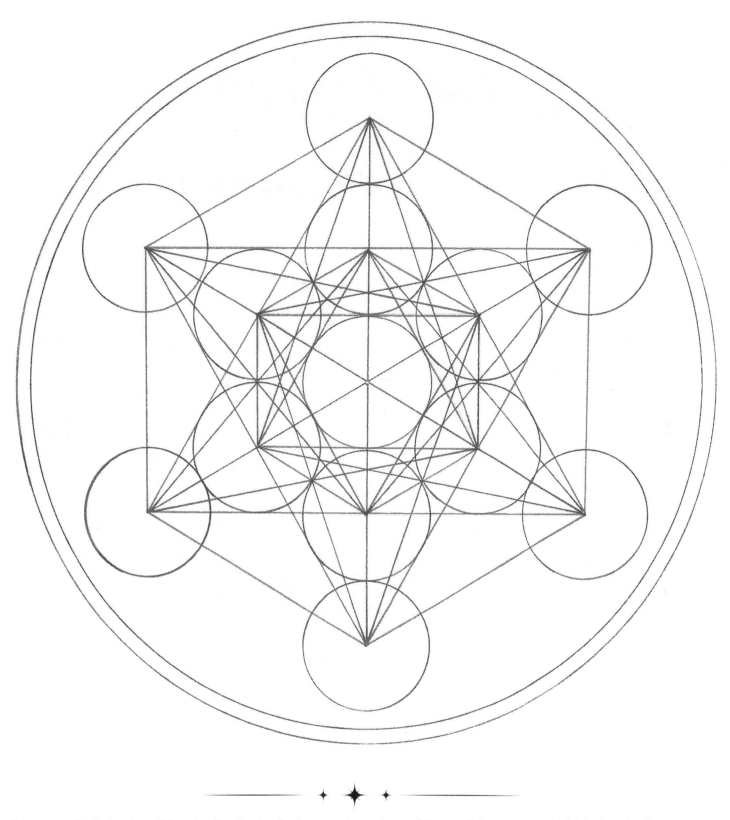

Metatron's Cube is said to be both the father and mother of Sacred Geometry. Within its design are 13 circles with lines connecting all of their centers. The patterns that emerge are a blueprint for creation, including the Platonic Solids and the harmonics of music.

Meditation: How can I realize that all knowledge exists within my very design?
How can I step into this power and live my full potential?

Affirmation: **I AM CONNECTED TO ALL THAT IS. I AM A TEMPLE OF DIVINE INFORMATION**.

I*nspiration: Ancient symbol with mysterious origins but is attributed to Fibonacci in the West.*

Blooming perennial flowers like narcissus, daffodils, and jonquils (to name a few) have six petals like this star glyph. This magical six-pointed star has infinite varieties while keeping the same underlying pattern.

Meditation: How can I compare my life to the lifecycle of a flower? Can I see the changing seasons of spring, summer, fall, and winter as times to bud, bloom, fade, go dormant, and sprout again?

Affirmation: **I AM ONE WITH THE ETERNAL CYCLE OF LIFE. I HONOR THE SEASONS AND EACH STAGE OF MY JOURNEY. I AM AN EXCEPTIONAL FLOWER OF CREATION.**

Inspiration: Geoglyph reported on July 8, 2017 at Hackpen Hill near Broad Hinton, UK.

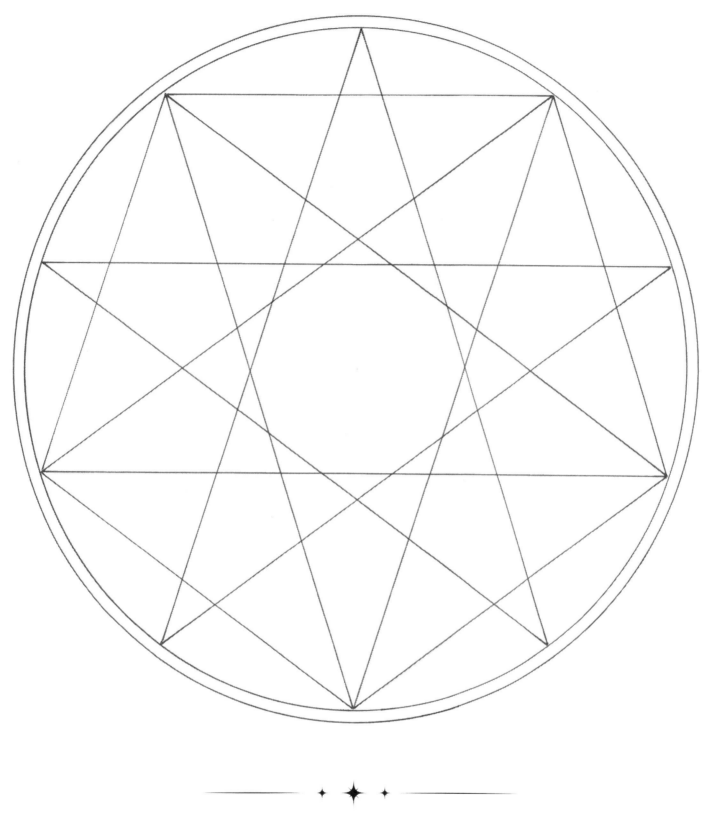

The PENTAGRAM has perfectly embedded in its design the PHI ratio of 1:1.618. This is the same proportion that occurs in our bodies – for example the relationship between our hand and our forearm. This ratio is found throughout nature, music, planetary orbits, and even stock market trends.

Meditation: How can I learn to see the patterns that exist all around me?
How can I realize the exquisite creation that is me?

Affirmation: **I AM BEAUTY. I AM HARMONY. I AM BALANCE. I AM LOVE.**

Inspiration: Geoglyph reported July 4, 2021 at Longwood Warren, Hampshire, UK.

The tetrahedron is one of the five Platonic Solids which are the building blocks of matter. It has four identical triangular faces – 3 that you can see and one underneath. It represents the element of fire.

Meditation: How can I connect to the fire within me? How can I bring my passion to life?

Affirmation: **I AM LIT BY AN INTERNAL FLAME OF CREATION.**
I LIVE MY PASSION EASILY AND EFFORTLESSLY.

Inspiration: Geoglyph reported on July 8, 2014 at Tetbury Lane, Wiltshire, UK.

Like ripples in a pond, our energy touches and overlaps with others, creating an "interference pattern" of geometric forms.

Meditation: What am I creating with those around me?
How can I co-create peace and harmony?

Affirmation: **I AM A DIVINE CREATIVE BEING.**
MY THOUGHTS AND ACTIONS SEND RIPPLES OUT INTO THE WORLD.

Inspiration: Geoglyph reported June 2, 2019 at Long Wood, Hampshire, UK.

When something is SQUARED, it's multiplied by itself, allowing it to jump to the next dimension. This star with 36 points is six times six or six squared. To reiterate this, the center circle contains repeating cubes.

Meditation: How am I multiplying myself? What are my thoughts and actions amplifying?

Affirmation: **I AM AN INSTRUMENT OF PEACE AND LOVE.**
I AM INCREASING THE POSITIVE VIBRATIONS ON THE PLANET.

Inspiration: Geoglyph reported August 1, 2007 at Sugarhill Aldbourne, Wiltshire, UK.

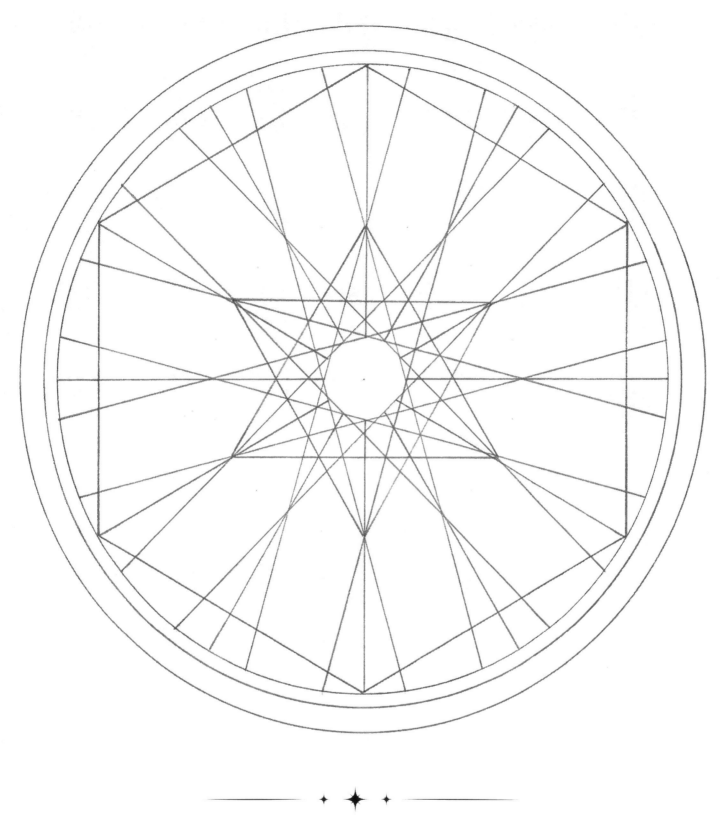

The 6-pointed star is a basic form of Sacred Geometry, symbolizing the MERKABA or Light Body. Also referred to as a star tetrahedron, it is held in a hexagon (6-sided shape) by what appears to be a net.

Meditation: How can I connect to my light body? How does my light connect to the environment around me? How can I become more conscious of the energy I project?

Affirmation: **I AM COMFORTABLE STANDING IN MY POWER AND KNOWING MY CONNECTION TO THE WORLD AROUND ME.**

Inspiration: Geoglyph reported July 14, 1997 at Cley Hill, Warminster, Wiltshire, UK.

In Sacred Geometry, the sphere represents the spirit (or unmanifested) while the cube represents the body or material world (manifested).

Meditation: How does my spirit show up in me? Is it fully animating my body or has it become overpowered by the material world? How can I balance the two?

Affirmation: **I AM A SPIRIT HAVING A PHYSICAL EXPERIENCE.**

Inspiration: Geoglyph reported July 19, 2015 at Ockley Hill, Surrey, UK.

When souls align with each other in a common mission or goal, they become larger and more powerful than one alone. Coming together with focused intention can help our vision grow and expand.

Meditation: Do I feel in alignment with my soul's mission?
Do I surround myself with like-minded people? Have I found my tribe?

Affirmation: **I AM ABLE TO FULFILL MY DREAMS.**
I AM ALIGNING WITH PEOPLE, PLACES, AND CIRCUMSTANCES NECESSARY TO REALIZE MY GOAL.

Inspiration: Geoglyph reported July 6, 2010 at Danebury Hill Fort, Hampshire, UK.

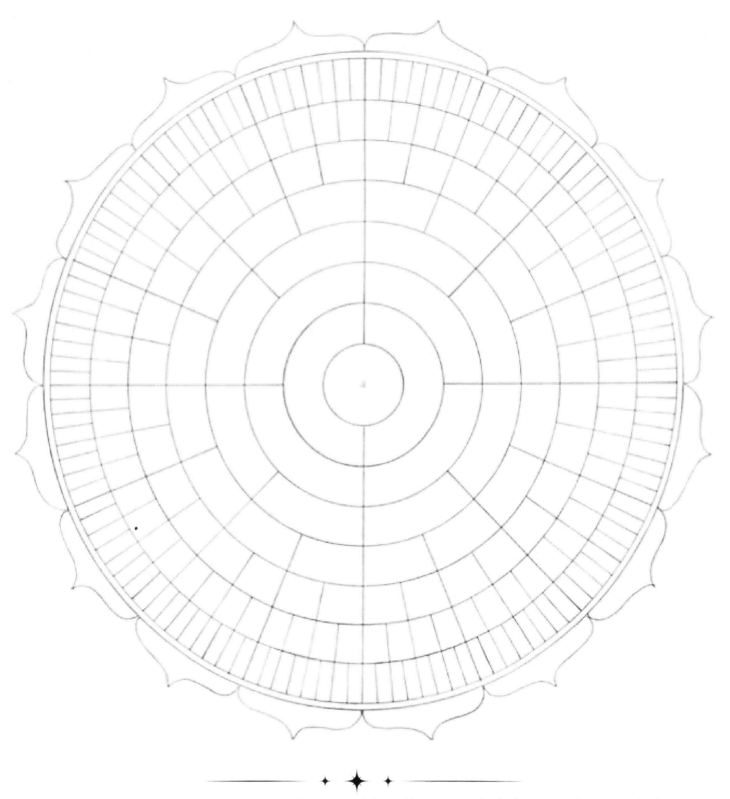

Concentric circles create a seven generation mandala. The center circle is YOU. The next circle out is split in two, representing your parents. The next circle is split in four, representing your parents' parents, and so on. When we view seven generations back in the outer ring, we have a total of 128 ancestors.

Meditation: How can I fully feel the support of my ancestors?
How can I realize the miracle of the very specific pairings that led to the creation of me?

Affirmation: **I AM A PERFECT & UNIQUE BEING, SURROUNDED BY THE POWER AND LOVE OF THOSE THAT HAVE COME BEFORE ME.**

Inspiration: Native American Generational Wheel.

Repeated geometric patterns have been found in many cultural traditions. They were used to adorn sacred places as well as everyday objects. Because they represent universal concepts that transcend language, they promote unity instead of division. Having these designs in our space promotes a feeling of calm and well-being, bringing us close to our source.

Meditation: What do I choose to surround myself with? Is my home full of calming patterns or chaotic designs? How do they make me feel?

Affirmation: **I AM ALWAYS SURROUNDED BY UNIVERSAL LOVE.
I AM OPEN TO RECEIVE THIS LOVE AND GUIDANCE.**

Inspiration: Geoglyph reported July 11, 2012 at Corley, Warwickshire, UK.

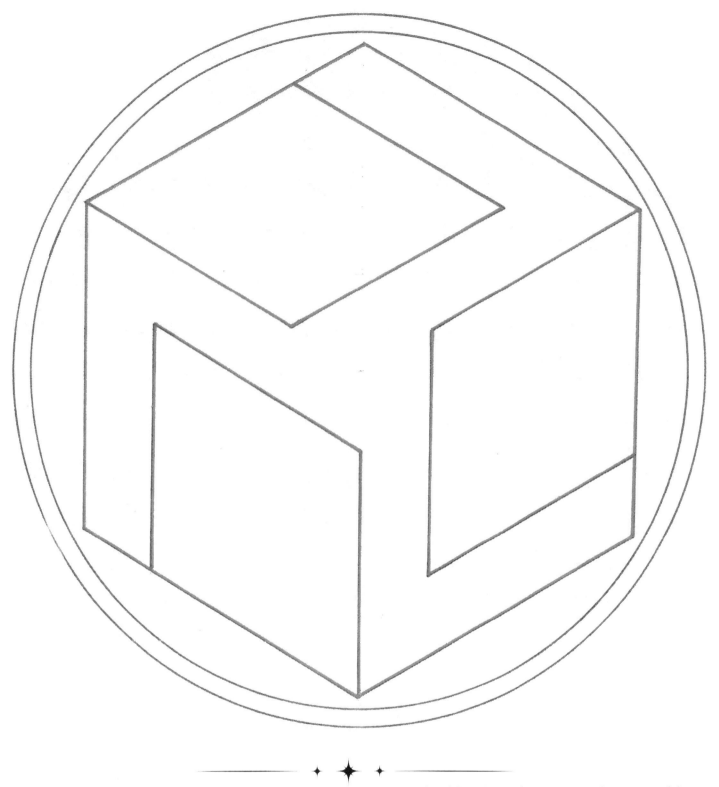

The Antakarana is a bridge to the higher self. In one perspective it's a 3D cube, connecting our spirit to the material world. In another perspective, it's three 7's representing the 7 chakras, the 7 colors, and the 7 notes of the musical scale. This symbol is used in the reiki tradition as a powerful healing tool, helping to neutralize negative energy, undo energy blockages, and restore a healthy flow.

Meditation: How can I connect to my higher self for wisdom and guidance?
How can I transmute negative energy into the purest version of myself?

Affirmation: **I AM CRYSTALIZED MUSIC AND COLOR.**
I AM THE DIVINE DANCE OF CREATION. I AM SAFE AND PROTECTED.

Inspiration: Ancient healing symbol used in China and Tibet for thousands of years.

The 64-tetrahedron grid represents the very fabric of spacetime, according to Nassim Haramein. It can infinitely expand and contract to create a stable flow of energy and can be seen as a shadow form of the 3D version of the Flower of Life.

Meditation: How can I feel my personal energy in perfect balance with all of life?
How can I see my breath as the expansion and contraction of the entire universe?

Affirmation: **I AM ONE WITH THE FABRIC OF LIFE. I AM FLOWING THROUGH SPACE AND TIME IN PERFECT HARMONY WITH ALL OF CREATION.**

Inspiration: Ancient symbol with mysterious origins

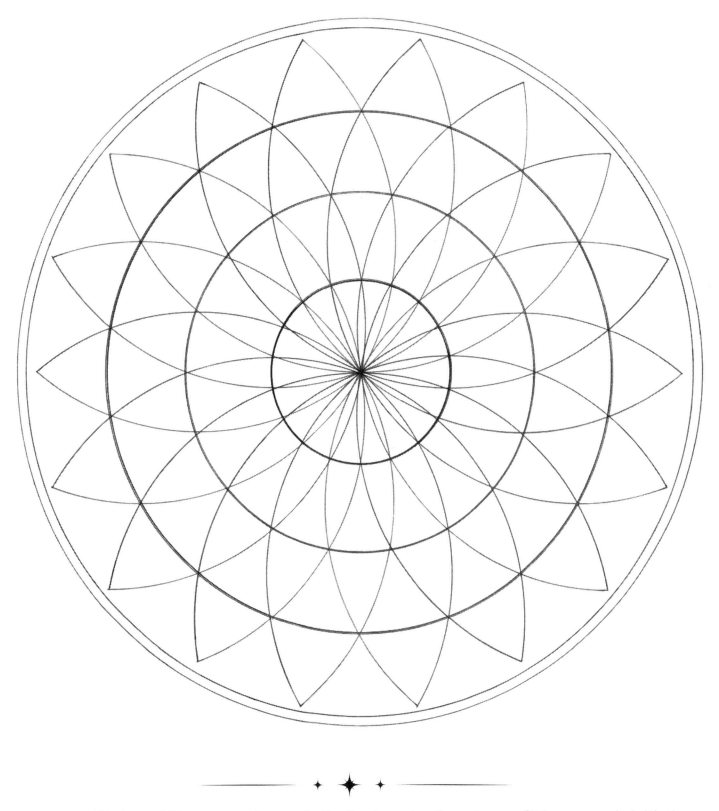

An average lifetime of 72 years can be symbolically viewed as four stages of 18 years each: initiation, planning, implementation, and closure. This flowering glyph has eighteen petals surrounding each concentric circle yet they are connected by an arc.

Meditation: How can I see my life as an arc of time that flowers from one stage to the next? How can I gracefully move through each point, knowing that all is in perfect order?

Affirmation: **I AM A FLOWERING OF LIFE. I AM A LIVING PATTERN OF CREATION.**

Inspiration: Geoglyph reported July 19, 2007 at Martinsell Hill, Wiltshire, UK.

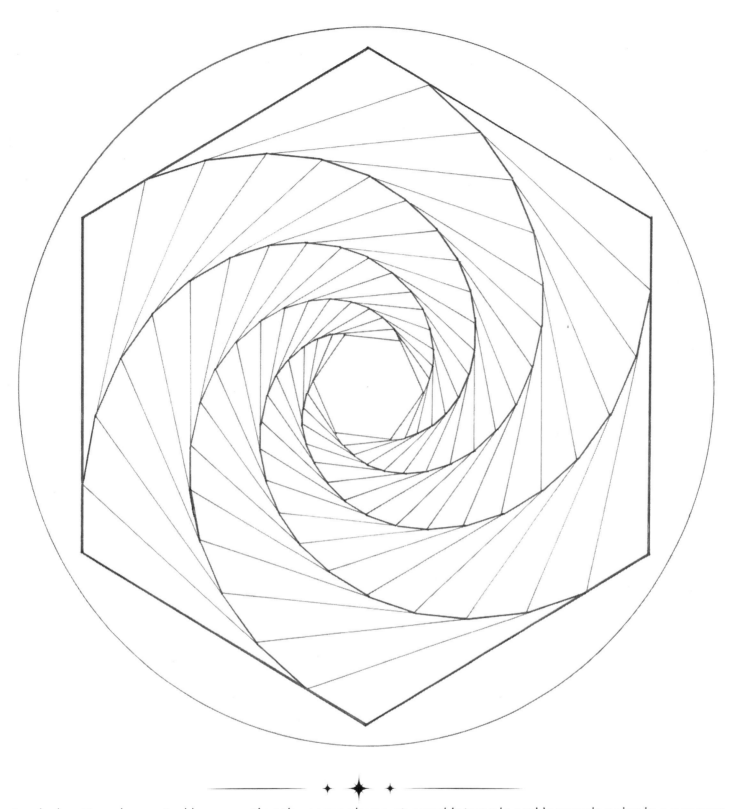

A spiral pattern is created by repeating the same shape at equal intervals and increasing size in a process called ratcheting. If you look closely you will see 19 hexagons starting from the center and ratcheting outward, creating interconnected spiral waves.

Meditation: How can I see the journey of life as an ever-expanding spiral that brings me around to the same situation from a different angle?

Affirmation: **I AM ETERNALLY GROWING AND EVOLVING WITH NEW INSIGHTS.
I AM JOYFULLY EXPANDING ALONG THE SPIRAL OF LIFE.**

Inspiration: Geoglyph reported July 2, 2021 at Avebury, Wiltshire, UK.

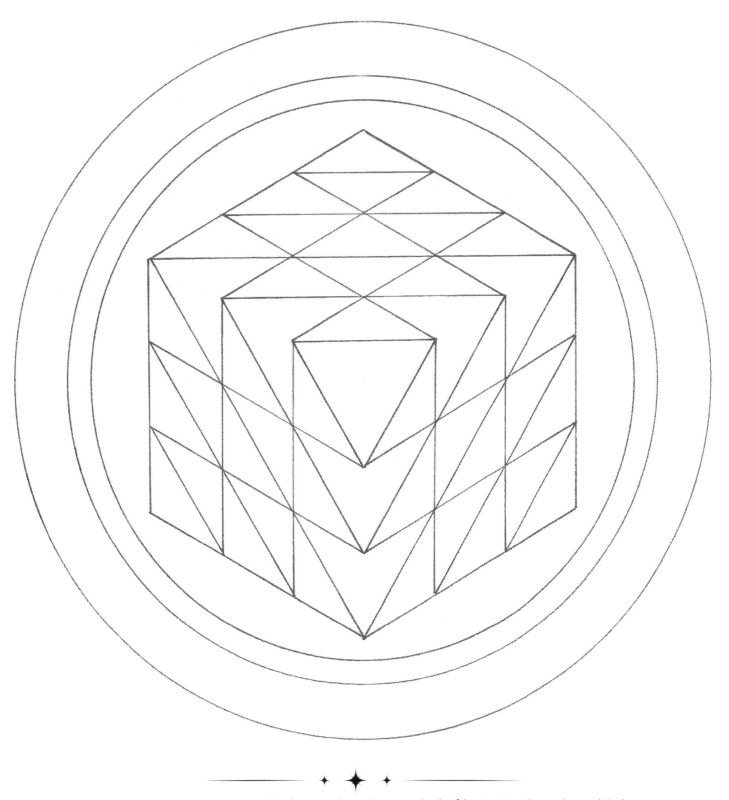

When a living creature is waiting to be born, there is a period of inCUBEation where it's kept warm. Warmth is symbolized by fire (the triangle in Sacred Geometry). This understanding can be extended to any creation like an idea, a plan, a work of art, etc.

Meditation: Am I keeping my ideas alive with the fire of passion?
How can I maintain the fire to help my creations be born?

Affirmation: **I AM CAPABLE OF BIRTHING ANY IDEA THAT I'M PASSIONATE ABOUT.
I SUSTAIN MY PASSION WITH FOCUSED INTENTION AND AWARENESS.**

Inspiration: Geoglyph reported July 16, 2019 at Fulley Wood, Hampshire, UK.

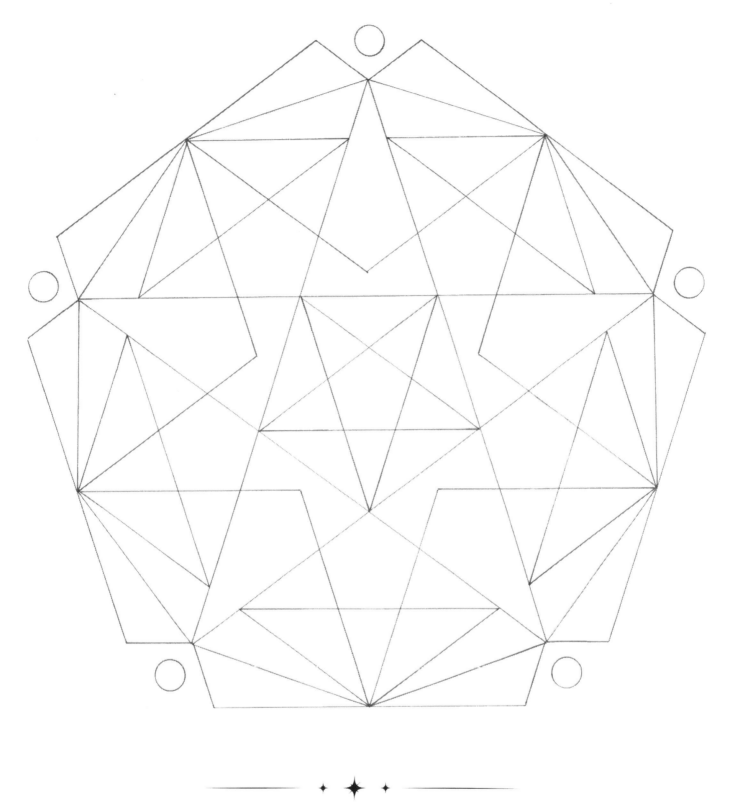

The five-pointed star (or pentagram) exhibits the same proportions as the human body. As the star is expanded, it's surrounded by a larger pentagram. The points of this star are formed into angels or higher beings holding hands (or wings) with the small circles as their heads.

Meditation: How can I feel the presence of angels surrounding and supporting me?
How can I see these higher beings as extensions of myself?

Affirmation: **I AM DIVINELY SUPPORTED AND PROTECTED.
I AM SURROUNDED BY ANGELS AT ALL TIMES.**

Inspiration: Geoglyph reported July 23, 2016 at Calstone Wellington, Wiltshire, UK.

Twenty-four emanations radiate out from this zig-zag star in 3 waves. A day in time contains 24 hours
with segments of morning, afternoon, and night.

Meditation: How does my energy change or switch direction at different times of day?
Can I recognize and be comfortable with this shifting?

Affirmation: **I AM AWARE OF MY DAILY ENERGY AND EASILY NAVIGATE THE HIGHS AND LOWS.
I AM COMFORTABLE WITH MYSELF AT ALL TIMES.**

Inspiration: Geoglyph reported August 9, 2020 at Uffington Castle, Oxon, UK.

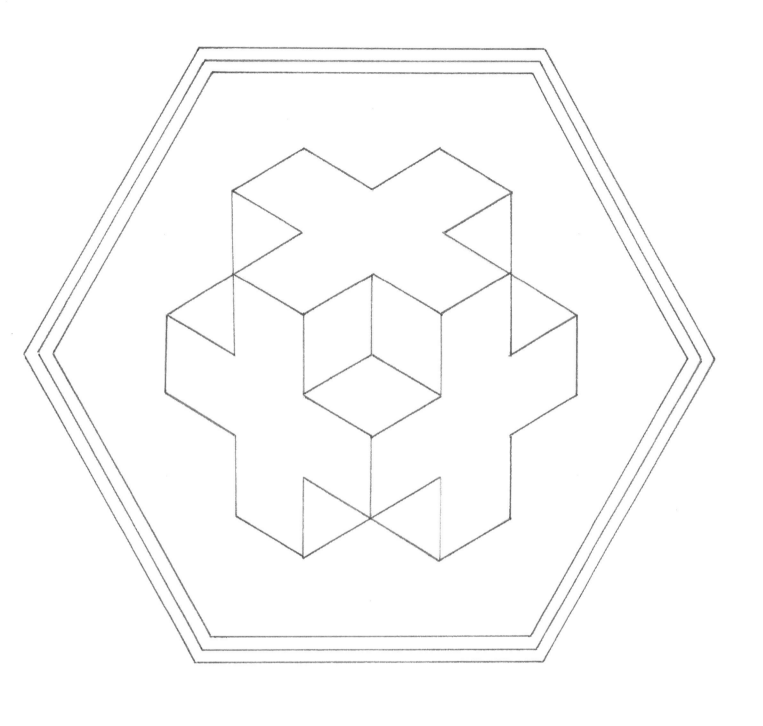

A cross is the union of the vertical spiritual energy with the horizontal physical plane. It represents the perfect balance of this union.

Meditation: How can I balance my spiritual life with my physical life?
How can I create the perfect union of spirit and matter?

Affirmation: **I AM A DIVINE SPIRITUAL BEING MANIFESTING IN THIS PHYSICAL BODY.
I PEFECTLY EMBODY MY SOUL IN THE HERE AND NOW.**

Inspiration: Geoglyph reported July 9, 2010 at Cley Hill, Wiltshire, UK.

The sun is a symbol of the burning light within each of us. Our sun gives life to all living things on the earth. The sun is the nucleus of our Solar System.

Meditation: How can I harness the power of the sun?
How can I connect to the eternal flame inside myself?

Affirmation: **I AM LIGHT. I AM LIFE.**

Inspiration: Geoglyph reported on August 15, 2021 at Roundway Hill, Wiltshire, UK.

The pentaGON (5-sided shape with equal sides) creates the pentaGRAM (5-pointed star) by connecting its corners. This shape can nest within itself infinitely smaller and expand to create itself infinitely larger.

Meditation: How can I see the external world as an expression of my core being?
How can I filter my mind so the outer world is a true reflection of my soul?

Affirmation: **I AM THAT. AS WITHIN, SO WITHOUT.**
I AM A UNIQUE EXPRESSION OF DIVINE LOVE, HARMONY, AND PROPORTION.

Inspiration: Divine guidance creating nine nesting pentagons.

An intricate eight-pointed star begins to display forms in nature like the tail of a whale or a bird opening its mouth. These patterns are repeated on all scales from micro to macro.

Meditation: How can I connect to nature and its wonders? Can I recognize patterns in the forms of nature? Can I see the perfection in this design?

Affirmation: **I AM INTIMATELY CONNECTED TO NATURE AND ITS PERFECT DESIGN.**

Inspiration: Geoglyph reported June 21, 2021 at Fulley Wood, Hampshire, UK.

In many traditions, to create a sacred circle, it is custom to call in the six directions of North, South, East, West, Above and Below.

Meditation:How can I create sacred space in my daily life?
How can I anchor myself in the here and now?

Affirmation: **I AM PRESENT IN THIS MOMENT IN TIME.
I AM STANDING IN SACRED SPACE.**

Inspiration: Geoglyph reported June 22, 2015 at Upper Rapeland, West Sussex, UK.

Three is the binding principle, like in a braid. It combines two opposite poles into a third thing that binds them together like father-mother-child, white-black-gray, left-right-center, blue-yellow-green, etc. The trinity knot isn't easily broken.

Meditation: How does the principal of three show up in my life? What binding relationships have I created with others? What relationship have I created with myself?

Affirmation: **I AM A FREE AND SOVEREIGN BEING. I AM ABLE TO MAKE CHOICES THAT ARE BENEFICIAL FOR MYSELF, MY FAMILY, MY COMMUNITY, AND MY WORLD.**

Inspiration: Geoglyph reported July 16, 2016 at Hackpen Hill, Wiltshire, UK.

A seven-pointed star can signify one week or 7 days. This star within a star is repeated four times, representing a lunar cycle of 28 days or 4 weeks.

Meditation: How does the moon affect my moods and emotions?
How can I become attuned to the power of the moon and its cycles?

Affirmation: **I AM PERFECTLY IN TUNE WITH NATURAL CYCLES AND RYTHMS.**

Inspiration: Geoglyph reported June 14, 2021 at Ludgershall, Wiltshire, UK.

The pentagram holds the ratios of our human bodies (as well as most animals and plants). Two sets of five create a symbol for how our bodies manifest our extremities with 2 sets of 5 fingers and toes.

Meditation: How can I appreciate the miracle of my body that allows me to interact with my environment in so many ways? Can I imagine how life would be different without these limbs that I so often take for granted?

Affirmation: **I AM A DIVINE GEOMETRIC BLUEPRINT OF CREATION. I AM PERFECTLY FORMED TO MAKE THE MOST OF THIS HUMAN EXPERIENCE.**

Inspiration: Geoglyph reported July 23, 2020 at Hackpen Hill, Wiltshire, UK.

The cube is one of the five Platonic Solids and represents the element of earth. Three cubes together appear as a six-pointed star, depending on the perspective they are viewed.

Meditation: How can I see things differently by changing my perspective? Is my experience of earth a joy or a tragedy? How can I shift my vision to create the life I desire?

Affirmation: **I AM THE CREATOR OF MY LIFE EXPERIENCE.**
I AM CAPABLE OF SHIFTING MY PERSPECTIVE TO REALIZE HEAVEN ON EARTH.

Inspiration: Geoglyph reported July 7, 2020 at Stanton St. Bernard, Wiltshire, UK.

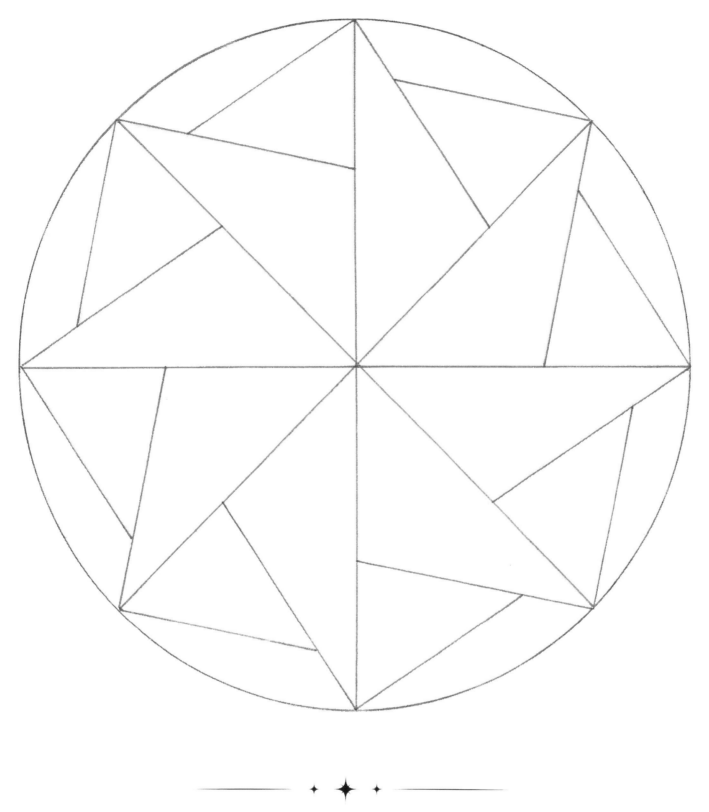

The number eight when placed on its side is the symbol for infinity. This 8-pointed star can be seen as a flower that is overlapping like an origami design, created from a single sheet of paper, having no beginning and no end.

Meditation: How can I feel the infinite nature of my existence? How can I tune into the past, present, and future as one continuous sheet of paper that is connected and overlapping?

Affirmation: **I AM AN INFINITE BEING WITH NO BEGINNING AND NO END.**

Inspiration: Geoglyph reported May 10, 2021 at Stanton St. Bernard, Wiltshire, UK.

The doubling or binary sequence is one of the patterns that creates life. The 8-pointed star (or octogram) in the center of this glyph is made with 2 overlapping squares of 4 corners each. It then expands out to 16 points around the outside, beautifully creating the binary sequence 2-4-8-16.

Meditation: How does doubling manifest in my own body? Is one side of me a reflection of the other? How can I integrate these two sides as a unique whole?

Affirmation: **I AM A UNIQUE AND MAGNIFICENT REFLECTION OF A DIVINE PATTERN. I AM MANIFESTING MY INDIVIDUALITY WITH JOY AND PURPOSE.**

Inspiration: Geoglyph reported July 3, 2011 at Temple Balsall, Warwickshire, UK.

A FRACTAL is an infinitely repeating pattern that is self-similar regardless of scale. This pentagram star glyph displays this similarity, containing many smaller pentagrams in its points. A fully colored version of this star is on the front cover of this book.

Meditation: How do the patterns of nature repeat themselves regardless of scale? How does the smallest atom resemble an entire galaxy? How do I fit into this pattern?

Affirmation: **I AM A PERFECT FRACTAL OF THE ENTIRE COSMOS.**
I AM THE LIVING UNIVERSE EMBODIED.

Inspiration: Geoglyph reported July 7, 2018 at Martinsell Hill, Wiltshire, UK.

A circle with twelve arms is reminiscent of a clock, dividing the day by hours. This circle is divided into 12 equal sections with six overlapping circles in the background.

Meditation: How is my time ordered? Does the day flow harmoniously? How can I create harmony between tasks and flow from one thing to the next?

Affirmation: **I AM A LIMITLESS BEING WITH THE ABILITY TO CREATE HARMONY IN THIS TIME EXPERIENCE**

Inspiration:Geoglyph reported on October 19/20, 2018 in Niederscherli, near Bern Switzerland.

A PARABOLA is a curved shape made from straight lines, giving the illusion of depth when drawn in 2D. The center of this six-pointed star appears to be a stretched triangle held in space, much like the unified field in which everything exists.

Meditation: How can I see through the illusion of what appears to be real in 3D? How can I open up my sixth sense to perceive other dimensions of existence?

Affirmation: **I AM COSMIC, EXISTING IN ALL DIMENSIONS AT ONCE. I AM ABLE TO ACCESS ANY PLANE OF AWARENESS BY MY DESIRE.**

Inspiration: Geoglyph reported June 25, 2012 at Cherhill, Wiltshire, UK.

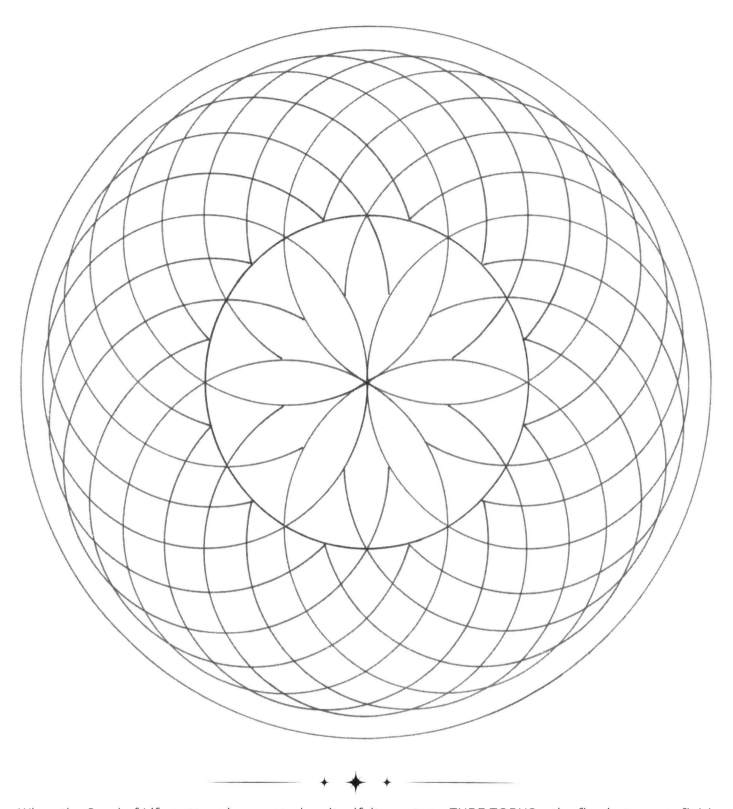

When the Seed of Life pattern is repeated on itself, it creates a TUBE TORUS – the flowing energy field around the human body. This torus pattern rotates and circulates our energy, traveling through the center, around the outside and back in, creating a dynamic exchange of power and momentum.

Meditation: Can I feel my energy field whirling around me?
Can I visualize this field flowing through me and spiraling out?
How can I consciously connect to this field and increase the flow to expand my energy and power?

Affirmation: **I AM A LIVING FIELD OF ENERGY. I AM POWERFUL BEYOND MEASURE.**

Inspiration: Flower of Life and tube torus patterns

Resources for Further Study

Access live links to videos & courses on my website:
PurpleLotusMosaics.com - LINKS
https://www.purplelotusmosaics.com/links

Recommended Reading:

The Ancient Secret of the Flower of Life, Vols. I & II
 By Drunvalo Melchizedek

Crooked Soley: A Crop Circle Revelation
By Allan Brown & John Michell

Crop Circles: The Bones of God
 By Michael Glickman

The Hidden Geometry of Flowers: Living Rhythms, Form and Number
 By Keith Critchlow

The Hidden Messages in Water
 By Masaru Emoto

Philomath: The Geometric Unification of Science & Art Through Number
 By Robert Edward Grant and Talal Ghannam, PhD

Sacred Geometry: Philosophy and Practice
 By Robert Lawlor

Secrets in the Fields: The Science and Mysticism of Crop Circles
 By Freddy Silva

Love & Gratitude

✦ ✦ ✦

My heartfelt thanks to you the reader – the artist of your own life – for choosing to grow and expand. When we heal ourselves, we heal the planet.

Infinite appreciation for my soulmate and partner Brad - for his constant love, encouragement, and support, and for his contagious energy. Thank you for following your dreams. Thank you for knowing I could realize mine.

Many many thanks to my daughter Becca for helping me create this book. Your imagination, technical skills, bright spirit, and kind wisdom were invaluable.

And ultimate gratitude and love to the Circlemakers. Your exquisite designs are an inspiration. And an Awakening.

Made in the USA
Columbia, SC
03 September 2024